Identify Your Skills for School, Work, and Life

Second Edition

by
J. Michael Farr
&
Susan Christophersen

JIST's Job Search Basics Series

Identify Your Skills for School, Work, and Life
Second Edition
© 1999 by JIST Works, Inc.

Previous edition published as *The Skills Advantage*

Published by JIST Works, Inc.
8902 Otis Avenue
Indianapolis, IN 46214
Phone: 1-800-648-5478   E-Mail: jistworks@aol.com

Visit our Web site for information on other JIST products: http://www.jist.com

Other books in JIST's Job Search Basics series
Two Best Ways to Find a Job, Second Edition
Introduction to Job Applications, Second Edition
Why Should I Hire You?: Turn Interview Questions into Job Offers, Second Edition
An instructor's guide for the series is available separately from JIST.

Development editor: Erik Dafforn
Editor: Susan Pines
Book design and layout: Aleata Howard
Cover design: Aleata Howard, Thomas R. Emrick

Printed in the United States of America

03 02 01 00 99   9 8 7 6 5 4 3 2 1

All rights reserved. No part of this book may be reproduced in any form or by any means, or stored in a database or retrieval system, without prior permission of the publisher except in case of brief quotations embodied in articles or reviews. Making copies of any part of this book for any purpose other than your own personal use is a violation of United States copyright laws.

We have been careful to provide accurate information throughout this book, but it is possible that errors and omissions have been introduced. Please consider this in making any career plans or other important decisions. Trust your own judgment above all else and in all things.

ISBN 1-56370-583-4

About This Book

This workbook will help you find a job. First, you will read about ideas that are important in the job-search process. Then you will interact with these ideas through questions and worksheets. Be sure to keep a pen or pencil handy! When you search for a job, remember what you learned here and look back through your answers as needed.

This book is one of four in JIST's Job Search Basics series. The following special features appear in the series:

Example. An "Example" usually features a conversation between two people about someone's struggles and successes in the job-search process. Learn what works—and what doesn't—with these real-world discussions. The photo that accompanies each "Example" will vary.

Think About It. It's time to stop reading when you see the lightbulb. Take a few minutes to think about what you just read. Answer the questions in the best way you can. Don't rush! When you are done writing, continue reading the book.

Notepad. This notepad image contains helpful information that is related to the main text. Be sure to pay attention to what you see on the notepads!

Worksheets. Worksheets are identified by the image at left. All worksheets contain clear directions to help you practice and interact with the concepts in the book.

Hints and Tips. These thoughts appear in the graphic you see at left. For extra guidance and inspiration, don't miss these boxes.

Checkpoint. When you see the clipboard, get ready to review the chapter. Answer the questions about the chapter's material. Look back and reread the pages as needed.

Challenge. The stopwatch means "stop and practice." Take your time and read each "Challenge." It will give you a chance to practice what the chapter teaches. Don't skip the "Challenge"! It's your chance to try out what you've learned before going out on a job search.

Good luck in your job search!

Other books in JIST's Job Search Basics series:

Two Best Ways to Find a Job, Second Edition

Introduction to Job Applications, Second Edition

Why Should I Hire You?: Turn Interview Questions into Job Offers, Second Edition

Table of Contents

INTRODUCTION 1

CHAPTER ONE: Taking Control of Your Life 3
   Are You Doing What Is Important to You? 4
   This Is Your Life 4
   What Does It Mean to Take Responsibility? 5
   Accepting Responsibility Is Good for You 6
   Your Time: Do You Spend It Well? 9
   Time-Tracking Worksheet 9

CHAPTER TWO: What Are Skills? 17
   Defining Skills 18
   Breaking Apart Your Skills 18
   Why Do You Need to Know Your Skills? 20
   Knowing Your Skills Helps You Choose Activities 21
      Choosing Activities That You Enjoy and Will Best Meet
         Your Needs 21
      Planning for Your Learning or Leisure Needs 22
      Using Your Best Skills to Get a Satisfying Job 22
   The Skills Triangle 23
      Adaptive Skills or Personality Traits 23
      Transferable Skills 24
      Job-Related Skills 24

© JIST Works, Inc., Indianapolis, IN

CHAPTER THREE: Identifying Your Adaptive and Transferable Skills 31

Your Adaptive and Transferable Skills 32
Your Adaptive Skills 32
Adaptive Skills Worksheet 33
Your Top Adaptive Skills 36
Adaptive Skills to Improve 37
Your Transferable Skills 37
Transferable Skills Worksheet 38
Your Top Transferable Skills 44
Transferable Skills to Improve 45

CHAPTER FOUR: Creating a Skills Inventory 51

Your Life Experience Can Help You Know Your Skills and Plan Your Career 52
Your Skills Inventory 52
Skills Inventory Worksheet 53
Your Top Skills 61
Things I Do Best 61
Skills I Most Enjoy Using 61
Skills I Most Want to Improve 62
Skills I Want to Use in My Next Job 62

CHAPTER FIVE: Planning on How to Best Use Your Skills 67

Making Your Inventory Work for You 68
My Best Skills 68

Jobs That Match Your Skills 68
Gathering Information 70
If You Need More Training or Skills 71
Formal Schooling 71
What Type of School Will Provide the Training You Need? 71
What Is the Reputation of the School? 72
How Will You Pay for It? 72
How Can You Arrange Your Schedule to Make Time for School? 72
What Sacrifices Are You Willing to Make for School? 72
What Is the Location of the School That Best Suits Your Needs? 73
The Military 73
On-the-Job Training 73
Apprenticeships 74
Self-Directed Training 74
Use Your Outer Resources 75
Use Your Inner Resources 76

Make a Plan 77
Goal Planning 78
Measure Your Progress 81

CONCLUSION: Skills for Life 87

INTRODUCTION

You already have hundreds of skills. For example, you can read this sentence, something that no other animal can do. Today you got up and got to wherever you are now, on your own, something that no machine or computer can do by itself.

You can think, make decisions, interact with people, follow instructions, solve problems, move objects, and do all sorts of things that science cannot yet duplicate. When you really think about it, the skills you have are amazing.

This book was written to help you understand the many skills you have or want to develop. It will also help you *use* these skills to make good decisions in your education, career, and life.

Chapter One

Taking Control of Your Life

THE GOALS OF THIS CHAPTER ARE

❏ To understand what it means to accept responsibility.

❏ To discover why taking responsibility helps you live a more satisfying life.

❏ To analyze how you spend your time.

Identify Your Skills for School, Work, and Life

Are You Doing What Is Important to You?

In this book, you will learn how to identify your key skills. These are your skills that you like to use and are good at. You will learn how to use these and other skills to help you succeed in school, in work, and in life.

But before you learn more about your skills, you should first think about what is most important in your life. You should also think about how you want to spend your time. That is what this chapter is about. Later, you can decide how to apply your key skills to activities where you want to spend your time.

This Is Your Life

Ask yourself these questions:

1. Whose life are you living?

2. Whose life should you be living?

3. Whose life do you want to be living?

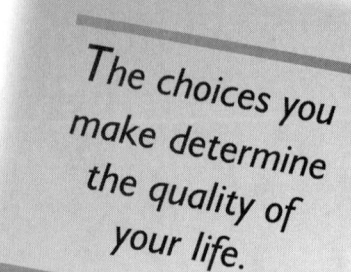

The choices you make determine the quality of your life.

Life is full of questions. The questions present choices. It's up to you to make the choices that work best for you.

No one knows you better than you know yourself. No one ever will. When it comes to your life, *you* are the expert.

Now answer these questions:

1. How can I create the best life possible for myself?

2. Do I feel I'm totally in control of my life?

Consider these questions carefully. Give them a lot of thought. They are some of the most important questions you will ever have to answer.

Chapter One: Taking Control of Your Life

Think About It

In the following spaces, write down some ideas about what you think it means to be totally in control of your life.

_____

_____

_____

_____

_____

_____

_____

_____

What Does It Mean to Take Responsibility?

Taking responsibility means that you:

- Don't blame anyone else for what happens to you.

- Don't try to control anyone else.

- Do take credit for what you do right.

- Do admit that you make mistakes.

- Do promise to learn from every mistake.

- Do consider the results of your actions before you act.

You take control of your life by taking responsibility for your life.

Learning to take responsibility for yourself is very hard. Everyone has problems with this at one time or another. Many people never learn to be completely responsible.

It is hard to be responsible, but it is worth the effort. In the following chapters, you'll see that accepting responsibility is a "key" skill—one that helps you get along in life.

It's better to make a new mistake than to keep making the old one.

Accepting Responsibility Is Good for You

When you accept responsibility for your life, you gain power. You are no longer under anyone else's control. Your thoughts are your own. Your feelings are your own. You own yourself.

When you blame other people for what happens to you or for how you feel, you lose power. You give it away. You're saying to those people, "You have more power over how I feel than I do. You have more power over what I think, and what happens to me, than I do."

What this means is that those people have control over you. Do you want other people to control your life? Or do you want to take control for yourself?

Accepting responsibility gives you the power to be in control of your own life. It frees you to make choices. It lets you take the opportunity to get what you need and want in your life—even if that means taking risks.

You might feel afraid of making choices and taking risks. Everyone does. But it's part of taking control. And taking control is one of the keys to living a truly satisfying life.

EXAMPLE: Learning to Take Responsibility

Susan and John are friends. They go to the same school, and they take many of the same classes. They even started working at a local flower shop at the same time.

Susan enjoyed working at the flower shop, but John did not. John didn't like taking orders, and he had trouble arriving at work on time. Eventually, John quit the job to look for an easier job.

Meanwhile, Susan enjoyed working at the shop, but she was having trouble with her job responsibilities. Her math skills were poor, and her supervisor was disappointed with the mistakes she was making with inventory and the cash register. Her supervisor told her that even though she had a good attitude, she would have to leave the job if she kept making mistakes.

Susan: So, John, how's the job hunt going?

John: Not very good. I almost had a job at the sporting goods store, but the boss wanted me to work both days on the weekends!

Susan: I really like my job at the flower shop, but I've been having some trouble with the math that it takes to do the work.

John: That's not your fault. Boy, those people really work you too hard!

Susan: They don't work me too hard. They just want me to make good business decisions and give the customers the correct change. After all, making too many mistakes could really hurt the profits. I would like to run my own business some day, and I wouldn't want someone working for me who makes math mistakes again and again.

John: Running your own business? Boy, that sounds like a real hassle! So how are you going to keep your job at the flower shop?

Susan: I enrolled in two night classes—one for business studies and the other for math.

(continued)

Example (continued)

John: You're taking business and math classes? Not me! I already took math. My math teacher was really bad. It's probably his fault I can't find a job!

Susan: When I took math before, I really wasn't concentrating very well. Some of it was hard, so I concentrated on other subjects. This time, at night school, it's going to be different.

Susan realized that only she could make a difference in developing her skills and being a good employee. She had made some mistakes in the past, but she took responsibility for them and corrected them.

John blamed others for his "bad luck." When something went wrong, he figured that there was no way he could change his situation.

Soon, Susan started making improvements in her job. The manager was impressed that she was learning additional business and math skills on her own. Susan worked very hard in her classes and eventually got a promotion.

John continued looking for a job without much luck. Every time he faced an opportunity, he found a reason to avoid it. He always had an excuse.

Think About It

In the following spaces, list the areas in your life where you want more control. It can be anything from finding the time to study more, to learning a new job skill, to eating the right foods.

_____

_____

_____

_____

_____

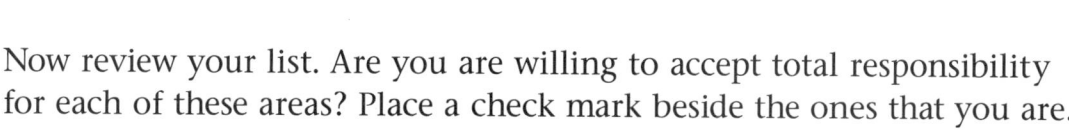

Now review your list. Are you are willing to accept total responsibility for each of these areas? Place a check mark beside the ones that you are.

Your Time: Do You Spend It Well?

Are you stealing from yourself? Time is like money. If you use it all up on things that aren't very important, you are cheating yourself. You don't gain anything of value.

You may own lots of things, but they don't mean much if you don't have the time to enjoy them. Or you may waste so much time that you don't do the things that are really important to you.

Time is precious. Wasting your time is like stealing your most valuable possession.

Time-Tracking Worksheet

During the next seven days, keep a record of how you spend your time. Use the "Time-Tracking Worksheet" on the next pages to see how you actually spend your time.

DIRECTIONS: In the "Activity" column, write down each activity you do that day. For example, "Ate breakfast," "Went shopping," "Went to work," "Watched TV," "Talked on the phone."

Identify Your Skills for School, Work, and Life

In the "Time" column, write down when you started the activity and when you stopped, as in "6:30–6:45 a.m.," "9:00–11:00 a.m.," and so on.

In the "Benefits to Me or Others" column, write how this activity helped or hurt you or someone else. It might have had good effects like "Helps me relax" or "Enjoyed time with a friend" or "Jogging keeps me in shape."

You may find that some activities do not help you. They may keep you from doing something more important, like studying or spending time with friends.

For example, spending three hours at night playing a computer game may "Keep me from reading." These notes will help you identify activities you want to change.

Time-Tracking Worksheet

Activity	Time	Benefits to Me or Others
Monday		

Chapter One: Taking Control of Your Life

Activity	Time	Benefits to Me or Others
Tuesday		
Wednesday		
Thursday		

(continued)

Identify Your Skills for School, Work, and Life

Time-Tracking Worksheet (continued)

Activity	Time	Benefits to Me or Others

Friday

Saturday

Chapter One: Taking Control of Your Life

Activity	Time	Benefits to Me or Others
Sunday		

Think About It

After you tracked your time for a week, what did you learn about yourself? How do you spend most of your time? Add up your time spent doing the same activity throughout the week.

In the left column on the next page, list the five activities in which you spent most of your time. In the right column, list the five activities you enjoyed doing the most. Compare the columns.

(continued)

Identify Your Skills for School, Work, and Life

Think About It *(continued)*

How I Spent the Most Time	What I Enjoyed Doing Most
1.	1.
2.	2.
3.	3.
4.	4.
5.	5.

Are you spending enough time on the things that are important to you? How could you spend more time on the things that matter the most to you? Write your notes on what you learned.

_____
_____
_____
_____
_____
_____
_____
_____
_____
_____
_____
_____

Chapter One: Taking Control of Your Life

Checkpoint

After completing this chapter, answer these questions. They will help you review what you learned. Your answers will also help you decide how you can use what you just learned.

1. How can you take control of your life?

_____

_____

_____

2. Why is it good for you to take responsibility for yourself?

_____

_____

_____

3. How do taking responsibility for yourself and the way you use your time relate to each other?

_____

_____

_____

4. How can you spend more time doing what you want to do and what you like to do?

_____

_____

_____

© JIST Works, Inc., Indianapolis, IN

Identify Your Skills for School, Work, and Life

CHALLENGE:
Develop Awareness of Responsibility and Time

Think of someone you know who complains often about "how life is treating" him or her. Then write answers to the questions below. (This exercise is not meant to criticize someone. But you can learn from looking at the behavior of others.)

1. Does this person seem happy? Why or why not?

   _____
   _____
   _____

2. Does this person blame other people for his or her situation in life? If so, what do you think of this?

   _____
   _____
   _____

3. Does this person take responsibility for his or her life? If so, how? If not, what makes you think this way?

   _____
   _____
   _____

Chapter Two

What Are Skills?

THE GOALS OF THIS CHAPTER ARE

- ❏ To understand what skills are.

- ❏ To see why knowing your skills can help you in your learning, career, and life.

- ❏ To learn about the kinds of skills that are most important to you.

Defining Skills

A skill is something you can do. Reading, writing, and cooking a meal are examples of skills. A skill can also be part of your personality. You might be skillful at getting along with others or good at organizing things.

Most activities require sets of skills that can be broken down into smaller skills. If you can learn to do the smaller skills, the whole activity becomes much easier to master.

Breaking Apart Your Skills

Driving a car is just one example of using many sets of skills in order to do an activity. Here are just some of the skills needed to drive a car:

- Reading road signs
- Eye-hand coordination
- Parallel parking
- Applying the brakes and accelerating correctly in different situations
- Understanding road maps and directions
- Concentrating
- Backing up
- Avoiding dangerous situations
- Knowing how to operate all controls
- Interpreting information from rearview mirrors

Chapter Two: What Are Skills?

As you can see, it takes many skills to drive a car. You may not realize how many skills you already have. Most people have hundreds of skills. You probably do, too. Does that surprise you? Like most people, you have probably developed some skills much more than others.

Think About It

Think about all the skills you use now. They can be skills you use in school, at work, at home, or elsewhere. Write them in the spaces below. You can list the same skill in more than one column.

School Skills	Work Skills	Leisure Skills

Which of these skills are you best at using? Place a check mark next to the skills you think you are best at. Which ones do you most like to use? Place a double check mark next to these skills.

The skills with the most check marks would be your best skills. However, you have many, many more skills, even if you haven't fully developed them yet.

Identify Your Skills for School, Work, and Life

Why Do You Need to Know Your Skills?

The things that you are good at and the things that you enjoy doing are an important part of who you are. Throughout our lives—in school, in work, and in our free or leisure time—our skills become a central part of our lives.

Your best skills are the ones you do well and enjoy using.

That is why you enjoy some school classes more than others. Whatever work we choose, we are happiest when we do work that is satisfying and meaningful to us. It may be unpaid work such as raising children, part-time work, or work that we have been trained and educated to do.

The same is true for how we spend our leisure time—we are happier when we spend time in ways that are satisfying and meaningful to us.

Think About It

1. What classes have you enjoyed the most?

   _____

   _____

   _____

2. What work do you enjoy doing so much that you would do it for free?

   _____

   _____

   _____

3. What things do you most like to do in your leisure time?

_____

_____

_____

_____

Knowing Your Skills Helps You Choose Activities

Listed below are several reasons why you need to know your skills:

- So you can choose activities that you enjoy and will best meet your needs.

- So you can best plan for your additional learning or leisure needs.

- So you can use your best skills to get a satisfying job.

Let's look at these reasons in more detail.

Choosing Activities That You Enjoy and Will Best Meet Your Needs

If you know what you are good at and enjoy doing, you are much more likely to do those activities. You won't waste time doing things that aren't important to you. Satisfaction in your life activities is directly related to using skills that you enjoy using. So it makes sense to know what those skills are.

Planning for Your Learning or Leisure Needs

If you are clear about what you enjoy, you can decide to learn more about a hobby, sport, or other activity you want to do. You could do the following:

- Read magazines or use the Internet to learn more.

- Join a club or team related to your interest.

- Talk to someone who enjoys this activity.

- Simply schedule more time in this activity.

Using Your Best Skills to Get a Satisfying Job

Knowing your skills is very important in deciding the type of job you want.

Whenever you go to a job interview, the most important question that you'll have to answer is "Why should I hire you?" Any employer is going to expect you to be able to answer that question.

You can't just say, "Because I'm a nice person" or "Because I really need to make some money." You'll have to convince an employer that you have the skills to do the job.

Many job applicants don't know how to do that. They don't know how to talk about their skills or their good worker traits.

Even though you have hundreds of skills, some will be more important to an employer than others. And some will be far more important to you as you decide what sort of job you want.

In the next section, you will learn about three major types of skills. This will help you prepare to use your best skills in planning your education, your career, your leisure time, and your life.

You have a better chance of being hired if you can communicate your skills to an employer.

The Skills Triangle

"The Skills Triangle" is a system that groups your skills into three major types. Most people don't think of the things they can do as skills. The Skills Triangle will help you remember the types of skills you have.

Later, knowing that you have a variety of skills will help you understand yourself—and better plan your education, your career, and your life.

Let's now learn more about each part of the Skills Triangle.

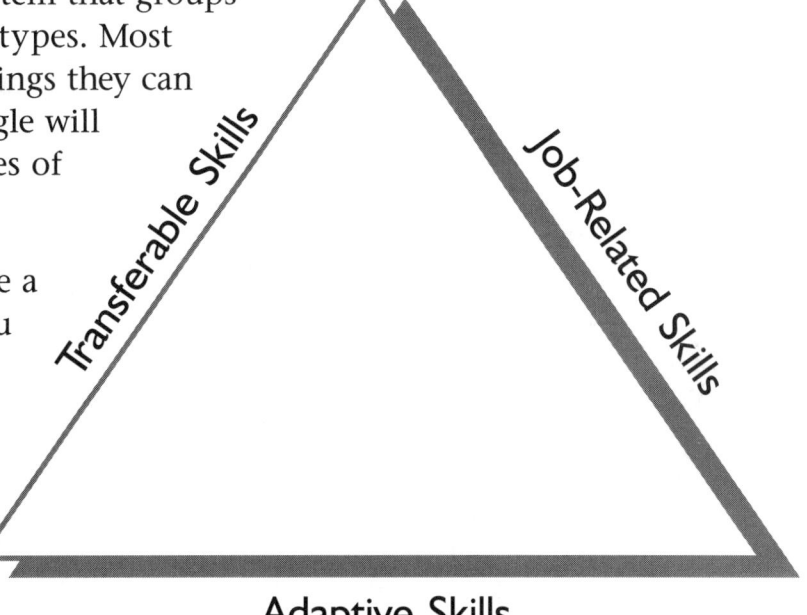

Adaptive Skills or Personality Traits

These are skills you use every day to survive and get along. They might be skills you have learned, or they could be part of your basic personality. Adaptive skills are also called self-management skills. They help you get along in different situations.

Some examples of adaptive skills are the following:

- Honesty
- Enthusiastic attitude
- Ability to follow instructions

Transferable Skills

These are general skills that can "transfer" from job to job. For example, good communication skills are useful in many different jobs. Transferable skills are very important to employers.

Some examples of transferable skills are as follows:

- Being able to manage people
- Solving problems
- Keeping track of money

Job-Related Skills

These are skills a person must know to do a specific job or type of job. The job can't be done without these skills. For example:

- An auto mechanic must know how to tune engines and repair brakes.
- A teacher must be able to present information in a way that students can understand.
- An administrative assistant must be able to use a computer and communicate well.

Chapter Two: What Are Skills?

Job-related skills are important, but they are not the most important thing that an employer considers. Often an employer will be willing to train an employee to learn the necessary job-related skills. The employee must have the right adaptive and transferable skills to get the job, but the job-related skills can sometimes be learned on the job.

The "Think About It" that follows shows why transferable and adaptive skills can get you hired for a job, even if you don't have all the job-related skills right now.

Think About It

Imagine that you are the manager of a local delivery company. You have one job opening and two job applicants to choose from. You are looking over your notes about each applicant. Here are your notes:

Applicant 1: Has experience as a delivery truck driver. Checked with previous employer. Was late for work fairly often. Missed some deliveries. Good driving record. Couldn't find location of delivery on several occasions, and left customers without supplies. Doesn't seem real motivated.

Applicant 2: No experience on this type of job. Previous employer says applicant hardly ever missed a day of work, was always on time, and dependable. Very enthusiastic. Seems eager to learn.

Which applicant would you hire? In the space that follows, explain why.

_____
_____
_____
_____
_____

(continued)

Identify Your Skills for School, Work, and Life

Think About It (continued)

___

___

___

___

Chances are, an employer will choose the same person for the same reasons you did. In the next chapter, you'll work with worksheets to identify your best skills of the three types in the Skills Triangle.

Checkpoint

After completing this chapter, answer these questions. They will help you review what you just learned.

1. What are skills? Give some examples of your skills.

___

___

___

___

2. How can knowing your skills help you find the job you want?

___

___

___

___

___

Chapter Two: What Are Skills?

3. Explain what the three types of skills are and tell which ones are most important to an employer.

_____
_____
_____
_____
_____

4. How can knowing your skills actually save you time?

_____
_____
_____
_____
_____

CHALLENGE:
Develop Your Skills Awareness

Think of a job that might interest you. Find out everything you can about the skills that are involved in doing that job. You can do this by talking to someone you know who does this job. You can go to the library and ask for a book on career information. You can search for the job on the Internet and connect to related sites.

(continued)

© JIST Works, Inc., Indianapolis, IN

Identify Your Skills for School, Work, and Life

CHALLENGE (continued)

Several books we recommend are the *Young Person's Occupational Outlook Handbook, Exploring Careers,* and the *Occupational Outlook Handbook.*

After you have gathered information about the skills needed, answer these questions:

1. What job-related skills do you already have for this job?

___

2. What job-related skills would you have to learn?

___

3. What transferable skills do you already have for this job?

___

Chapter Two: What Are Skills?

4. What adaptive skills do you already have for this job?

_____
_____
_____
_____
_____
_____
_____
_____
_____

Chapter Three

Identifying Your Adaptive and Transferable Skills

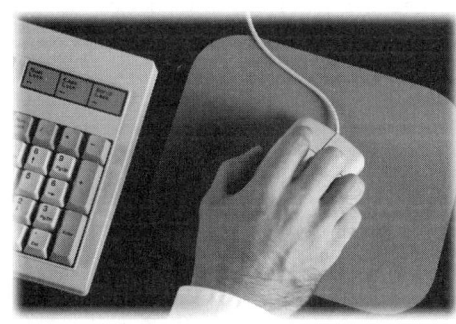

THE GOALS OF THIS CHAPTER ARE

❏ To identify your skills.

❏ To understand how you can use your skills in learning, career, leisure, and life planning.

❏ To begin learning how to communicate those skills.

Your Adaptive and Transferable Skills

In Chapter Two, you learned about three types of skills. They are as follows:

- Adaptive skills/personality traits
- Transferable skills
- Job-related skills

When you identify your best skills in each of these groups, you can do the following:

- Make good decisions about your learning, career, and leisure options.
- Answer the most important question an employer will ask: "Why should I hire you?"

Your Adaptive Skills

On the following lines, list three things about yourself that help you get along in life or that make you a "good" person. Take your time.

1. _____
   _____
   _____

2. _____
   _____
   _____

Chapter Three: Identifying Your Adaptive and Transferable Skills

3. _____
   _____
   _____

These three traits may be some of the most important things you need to know about yourself. They define the way you see yourself and what you have to offer others.

Many people think these skills or traits are not important enough to talk about, but they are. In a job interview, for example, mentioning these traits may get you hired over someone who actually has more experience than you do.

Adaptive Skills Worksheet

The worksheet that follows contains a list of adaptive skills. The first group of skills—"Basic Adaptive Skills"—is the most important one. Many employers will not hire an applicant who does not have these skills. The second group of skills is important for many jobs.

DIRECTIONS: Look over the list and put a check mark beside any skill that you feel you have now. In the "Want to Improve" column, put a check mark beside any skill that you feel you need to improve. (Later in this book we will go over ways to develop and improve your skills.)

At the end of the worksheet, you can add other skills that you feel you have now or want to improve that are not listed here.

© JIST Works, Inc., Indianapolis, IN

Identify Your Skills for School, Work, and Life

Adaptive Skills Worksheet

Basic Adaptive Skills

Adaptive Skill	Have Now	Want to Improve
Good attendance		
Honest		
Arriving on time		
Following instructions		
Meeting deadlines		
Hard working		
Getting along with others		

Other Adaptive Skills

Skill	Have Now	Want to Improve
Ambition		
Patience		
Flexibility		
Maturity		
Assertiveness		
Dependability		
Learn quickly		
Complete assignments		

Other Adaptive Skills

Skill	Have Now	Want to Improve
Sincerity		
Motivation		
Problem solving		
Friendliness		
Sense of humor		
Leadership		
Physical stamina		
Enthusiasm		
Good sense of direction		
Persistence		
Self-motivated		
Accept responsibility		
Results oriented		
Willing to ask questions		
Pride in doing a good job		
Willing to learn		
Creative		

(continued)

Adaptive Skills Worksheet (continued)

More Adaptive Skills (Add your own.)

Skill	Have Now	Want to Improve

Your Top Adaptive Skills

Review your list of adaptive skills. Then, in the spaces below, list the three adaptive skills that you feel are most important for an employer to know about you.

1. _____
2. _____
3. _____

Adaptive Skills to Improve

Now list the three adaptive skills that you feel are the most important ones for you to work on improving. (Keep these in mind for later. We'll work on improving skills in a later chapter.)

1. _____
2. _____
3. _____

Your Transferable Skills

Adaptive skills are more like "personality traits" or "who you are," while transferable skills, like being organized, are "things you do." Many skills, like "accept responsibility," could be put into either group. Don't worry about this in making your lists. There is some overlap, and it just isn't that important to worry about.

Remember:
- *Adaptive skills are more like "who you are."*
- *Transferable skills are "things you do."*
- *Some skills can go into either group.*

On the lines below, list three of your transferable skills. Remember, these are the skills that you can take with you from job to job. It is important for you to know these skills so you can share them with a potential employer.

1. _____
2. _____
3. _____

Identify Your Skills for School, Work, and Life

There are hundreds of transferable skills. The worksheet that follows includes the ones that are most important to employers. Are the skills you listed included on the worksheet?

Transferable Skills Worksheet

The skills on this worksheet are organized into clusters. This is to help you identify major types of jobs that will suit you best.

DIRECTIONS: Read the list and put a check mark beside each skill that you feel you are strong in. Then go through the list again and put another check mark in the "Use in Next Job" column if you think you want to use that skill in your next job.

Note: Jobs that tend to pay more or have more responsibility often require one or more of the "key" skills at the beginning of the worksheet. If you have any of these skills, you will want to emphasize them to potential employers.

Transferable Skills Worksheet

Key Transferable Skills (These are very important to employers.)		
Skill	Already Strong	Use in Next Job
Meeting deadlines		
Planning		
Public speaking		
Budgeting and money management		

Key Transferable Skills (These are very important to employers.)

Skill	Already Strong	Use in Next Job
Supervising others		
Instructing others		
Accepting responsibility		
Managing people		
Meeting the public		
Working effectively in a group		
Organizing projects		
Taking risks		
Self-controlling		
Self-motivating		
Detail oriented		
Knowledge of basic computer skills		
Can explain things to others		
Problem solving		
Good writing skills		
Good math skills		

(continued)

Transferable Skills Worksheet (continued)

Other Transferable Skills: Working with Things

Skill	Already Strong	Use in Next Job
Using my hands		
Assembling things		
Building things		
Constructing, repairing buildings		
Making things		
Observing, inspecting things		
Driving or operating vehicles		
Operating tools and machinery		
Using complex equipment		

Other Transferable Skills: Working with Data

Skill	Already Strong	Use in Next Job
Analyzing data, facts		
Auditing records		
Investigating		
Using the Internet		
Sending and receiving e-mail		

Other Transferable Skills: Working with Data

Skill	Already Strong	Use in Next Job
Researching and locating information		
Calculating, computing		
Classifying data		
Counting		
Observing		

Other Transferable Skills: Working with People

Skill	Already Strong	Use in Next Job
Patient		
Sensitive		
Social		
Tactful		
Teaching		
Interviewing others		
Listening		
Tolerant		
Understanding		

(continued)

Transferable Skills Worksheet (continued)

Other Transferable Skills: Working with People

Skill	Already Strong	Use in Next Job
Kind		
Diplomatic		
Counseling people		
Confronting (when necessary)		
Trusting		
Can be firm		

Other Transferable Skills: Using Words and Ideas

Skill	Already Strong	Use in Next Job
Can be logical		
Speaking in public		
Designing		
Editing		
Remembering information		
Writing clearly		
Corresponding with others		
Creative		

Chapter Three: Identifying Your Adaptive and Transferable Skills

Other Transferable Skills: Using Leadership Ability

Skill	Already Strong	Use in Next Job
Arranging social functions		
Competitive		
Motivating people		
Can be decisive		
Running meetings		
Delegating		
Working out agreements		
Planning		

Other Transferable Skills: Using Creative, Artistic Ability

Skill	Already Strong	Use in Next Job
Dancing, body movement		
Drawing, art		
Performing, acting		
Playing instruments		
Presenting artistic ideas		
Music appreciation		
Expressive		

(continued)

Identify Your Skills for School, Work, and Life

Transferable Skills Worksheet (continued)

Other Transferable Skills: Add Your Own

Skill	Already Strong	Use in Next Job

Your Top Transferable Skills

Review your worksheet of transferable skills. List the five that you are best in or that are most important to you below.

1. _____
2. _____
3. _____
4. _____
5. _____

Chapter Three: Identifying Your Adaptive and Transferable Skills

Transferable Skills to Improve

Now list the five skills you most want to improve. (We'll work on improving your skills later in this book.)

1. _____
2. _____
3. _____
4. _____
5. _____

In the next chapter, you will create an "inventory" of your experiences. This listing of experiences can be used to help you uncover even more skills, including job-related skills.

Checkpoint

After completing this chapter, answer these questions. They will help you review what you just learned.

1. What are adaptive skills?

_____
_____
_____

2. What are transferable skills?

_____
_____
_____

(continued)

© JIST Works, Inc., Indianapolis, IN

Identify Your Skills for School, Work, and Life

Checkpoint *(continued)*

3. Why is it so important for you to know and be able to communicate your adaptive and transferable skills?

Notes

Write down any questions you have about what you read. Or make notes about points you want to remember.

Chapter Three: Identifying Your Adaptive and Transferable Skills

CHALLENGE:
Practice Communicating Your Skills

Look back at the three top adaptive skills that you listed. Think about situations in your life when you used each of those skills. Briefly describe those situations and how you used the skills. Can you support your claim that you have these skills? (This becomes very important during job interviews.)

Adaptive Skill 1

_____

_____

How I used this skill:

_____

_____

_____

(continued)

CHALLENGE (continued)

_____
_____
_____
_____

Adaptive Skill 2

_____
_____

How I used this skill:

_____
_____
_____
_____
_____
_____

Adaptive Skill 3

_____
_____

Chapter Three: Identifying Your Adaptive and Transferable Skills

How I used this skill:

_____

_____

_____

_____

_____

_____

_____

_____

_____

_____

Chapter Four

Creating a Skills Inventory

THE GOALS OF THIS CHAPTER ARE

❏ To create a skills inventory using your life history.

❏ To use your skills inventory to support your key skills.

❏ To use your skills inventory to identify job-related skills.

❏ To use your skills inventory to plan education, career, or leisure activities.

Your Life Experience Can Help You Know Your Skills and Plan Your Career

In Chapter Three, you used worksheets to identify your adaptive and transferable skills. These were two of the types of skills from the Skills Triangle.

In this chapter, you will be gathering information about yourself from all the experiences that you have had. In these experiences are keys to two important considerations:

- Who you are.

- What you have spent time and effort on.

These are also keys to what you do well now and what you are likely to do well in the future.

Your Skills Inventory

Completing the worksheets that follow will help you form a skills inventory. With this inventory, you will see that many of your life experiences can support your adaptive and transferable skills. The inventory can also help identify your job-related skills, the third group of skills from the Skills Triangle.

Chapter Four: Creating a Skills Inventory

Job-related skills don't just come from jobs you have had or have been trained for. You probably have many skills that you have developed through a variety of activities.

The skills inventory you put together in this chapter will be very important to your career and life planning.

This knowledge can be used to help you make good decisions about your career, more education, or how you spend your leisure time. And it can help you get a good job. For example, you have a better chance of convincing an employer to hire you when you can prove your skills.

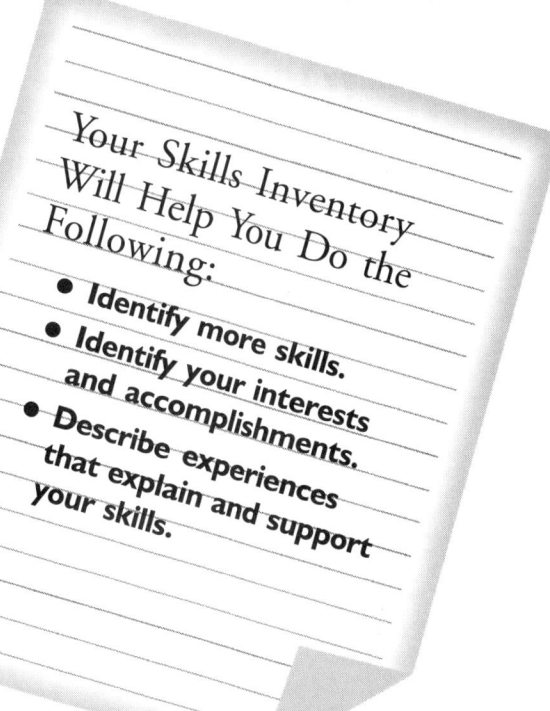

Your Skills Inventory Will Help You Do the Following:
- Identify more skills.
- Identify your interests and accomplishments.
- Describe experiences that explain and support your skills.

Skills Inventory Worksheet

DIRECTIONS: Complete the worksheet that follows to target the key experiences and skills you gained through education, work, volunteer activities, and other experiences.

The worksheet asks you to list in the left column things you studied or did, and in the right column, skills you strengthened or gained as a result. For example, one young man listed his literature class on the left. On the right, he noted:

"Big help to me in learning to think and write. I even learned to analyze situations and how other people solved problems. My reading and communications skills got better, too."

Education and Training

Junior High School

On the lines below, include coursework that relates to your job interests.

Subjects Studied	Skills Strengthened or Gained

On the lines below, include any special organizations that you participated in, whether in or out of school. These might be clubs, teams, hobby groups, and so on.

Extracurricular Activities	Skills Strengthened or Gained

Chapter Four: Creating a Skills Inventory

High School

On the lines below, include coursework that relates to your job interests.

Subjects Studied	Skills Strengthened or Gained

On the lines below, include any special organizations that you participated in, whether in or out of school. These might be clubs, teams, hobby groups, and similar groups.

Extracurricular Activities	Skills Strengthened or Gained

(continued)

Education and Training (continued)

After High School

In this section, list any education or training you had after high school. Include training you have received in the military, if any.

Subjects Studied	Skills Strengthened or Gained

In this section, list activities and organizations that you participated in.

Activities	Skills Strengthened or Gained

Work History

For this section, you will list all the jobs you've had and what your responsibilities were. In the right column, list the skills you strengthened or gained. Include part-time jobs, summer jobs, or self-employment like mowing lawns or babysitting.

Job and Responsibilities	Skills Strengthened or Gained

Job and Responsibilities	Skills Strengthened or Gained

Job and Responsibilities	Skills Strengthened or Gained

(continued)

Work History (continued)

Job and Responsibilities	Skills Strengthened or Gained

Volunteer Experience

You don't have to have been paid for work to have valuable work experience. In this section, list any volunteer work you have done, and the skills you strengthened or gained while doing it.

Volunteer Job and Responsibilities	Skills Strengthened or Gained

Volunteer Job and Responsibilities	Skills Strengthened or Gained

Chapter Four: Creating a Skills Inventory

Volunteer Job and Responsibilities	Skills Strengthened or Gained

Volunteer Job and Responsibilities	Skills Strengthened or Gained

Hobbies, Leisure Activities, and Other Life Experiences

For this section, list hobbies, special interests, family activities, or any other activities that have led you to develop specific skills. Take plenty of time to think and remember. As we said earlier in this book, you have many more skills than you realize!

(continued)

Identify Your Skills for School, Work, and Life

Hobbies, Leisure Activities, and Other Life Experiences (continued)

For example, maybe you help take care of the younger children in your family. Doing this would help you gain skills in child care, patience, taking responsibility, food preparation, and other areas.

If you like to use your computer at home, you may have gained skills in using the Internet to find information, keyboarding and word processing, or Web page design.

Special Activity	Skills Strengthened or Gained

Special Activity	Skills Strengthened or Gained

Special Activity	Skills Strengthened or Gained

Chapter Four: Creating a Skills Inventory

Special Activity	Skills Strengthened or Gained

Your Top Skills

Now you will need to go back over the entire worksheet you just completed. Use each section to complete the lists that follow here.

Things I Do Best

1. _____
2. _____
3. _____
4. _____
5. _____

Skills I Most Enjoy Using

1. _____
2. _____

3. _____

4. _____

5. _____

Skills I Most Want to Improve

1. _____

2. _____

3. _____

4. _____

5. _____

Skills I Want to Use in My Next Job

1. _____

2. _____

3. _____

4. _____

5. _____

Congratulations! You now have an inventory to help you make valuable decisions about your life and your work.

Don't worry about figuring out your entire life goals right now. People grow and change throughout their lives, and you are bound to change, too. You can't predict the future. So make the decisions that make sense now. That's the best anyone can do.

Chapter Four: Creating a Skills Inventory

Checkpoint

After completing this chapter, answer these questions. They will help you review what you just learned.

1. Were you surprised by how many skills you have acquired from your experiences? What surprised you the most?

_____
_____
_____
_____
_____

2. How can you best use your skills inventory to get a job?

_____
_____
_____
_____
_____

3. Think of a job you might want to apply for. If you were an employer, would you hire yourself for this job? What skills do you need to work on to give yourself the best chance of getting the job?

_____
_____
_____
_____
_____

© JIST Works, Inc., Indianapolis, IN

Identify Your Skills for School, Work, and Life

CHALLENGE:
Think About Career Options

Have you ever dreamed of being your own boss? This could be a real option for you. Look over your skills inventory and think about the activities you enjoy the most. You might be able to combine your skills and interests to start a business of your own.

Hobbies such as gardening can turn into a landscaping business, for example. If you like woodworking, you could do furniture repair and refinishing. If you know a lot about computers, you could have a computer repair or consulting business. Some of the skills required to be self-employed are the following:

- Time management
- Marketing your service or product
- Self-discipline and motivation
- Money management
- Willing to work hard
- Locating necessary supplies or equipment
- Serving customers

Can you think of some others? Write them here:

_____

_____

_____

Chapter Four: Creating a Skills Inventory

_____

_____

_____

Self-employment is just one of many ways you can put your skills to work doing what you like to do. Becoming self-employed is not easy and may require a lot of preparation and work.

If you think you are interested in self-employment, many good resource books and other information are available in the library and on the Internet. If you are interested, we suggest you learn as much as you can about self-employment or starting a business.

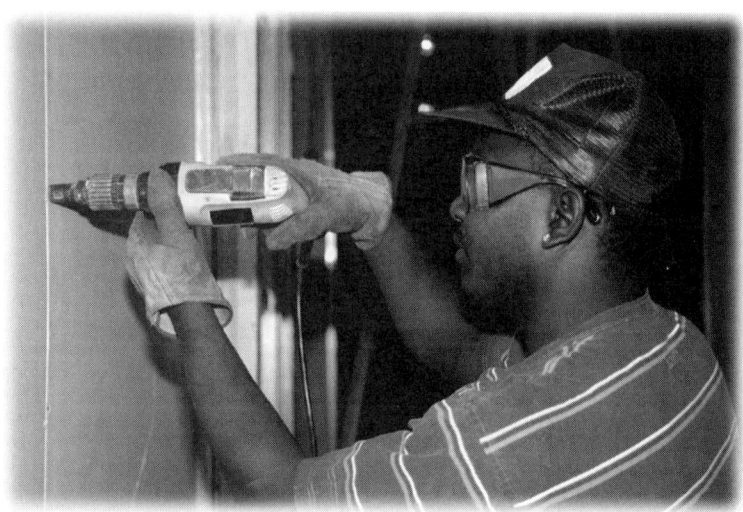

Chapter Five

Planning on How to Best Use Your Skills

THE GOALS OF THIS CHAPTER ARE

❏ To learn how to gather information about jobs that match your skills.

❏ To find out ways to develop more skills.

❏ To consider options for additional education or training.

Making Your Inventory Work for You

In the last chapter you spent considerable time creating an inventory of your skills and experiences. In this chapter you will learn how to use this inventory to determine which careers would be best suited to your skills. You will also learn to identify resources for further education or training.

My Best Skills

Go back through Chapters Three and Four to review the skills you identified as your best skills. These are the skills that you do well and may want to use in your next job. Write them again here.

Transferable	Adaptive	Job-Related

Jobs That Match Your Skills

There are thousands of job titles. Yet your task is to select just a few jobs that best fit your skills and interests. One way to do this is to consider groups of similar jobs.

The list below provides groups of jobs organized into 12 major clusters of interest areas. Later, you can go to a library and look up the jobs in the clusters. For now, just check the clusters of jobs that sound most interesting to you.

____ 01 **Artistic**. An interest in the creative expression of feelings or ideas.

____ 02 **Scientific**. An interest in discovering, collecting, and analyzing information about the natural world, and in applying scientific research findings to problems in medicine and the natural sciences.

____ 03 **Plants and Animals**. An interest in working with plants and animals, usually outdoors.

____ 04 **Protective**. An interest in using authority to protect people and property.

____ 05 **Mechanical**. An interest in applying mechanical principles to practical situations by use of machines or hand tools.

____ 06 **Industrial**. An interest in repetitive, concrete, organized activities done in an industrial or factory setting.

____ 07 **Business Detail**. An interest in organized, clearly defined activities requiring accuracy and attention to details, primarily in an office setting.

____ 08 **Selling**. An interest in bringing others to a particular point of view by personal persuasion, using sales and promotional techniques.

____ 09 **Accommodating**. An interest in catering to the wishes and needs of others, usually on a one-on-one basis.

____ 10 **Humanitarian**. An interest in helping others with their mental, spiritual, social, physical, or vocational needs.

____ 11 **Leading-Influencing**. An interest in leading and influencing others by using high-level verbal or numerical abilities.

____ 12 **Physical Performing**. An interest in physical activities performed before an audience.

Identify Your Skills for School, Work, and Life

Gathering Information

You will probably need more information to identify the jobs that interest you. You need to know about required skills and needed training or education. There may be jobs that match your skills and interests that you haven't thought of yet.

Here are some ways to find out more about the jobs that interest you.

1. Go to your public library and look up information in the following publications. (You can ask the librarian to help you find these and other resources.)

    ■ *Occupational Outlook Handbook:* Published by the U.S. Department of Labor, this book provides good descriptions of the top few hundred jobs in this country. It includes information on the nature of work, average pay rates, education and training required, projections for growth, and many other details.

    ■ *Young Person's Occupational Outlook Handbook*: Covers all the jobs in the *Occupational Outlook Handbook* in an easy-to-understand format.

    ■ *Exploring Careers:* Written for young people, this book describes jobs in major clusters, featuring people who actually work in the jobs in some of the descriptions.

    ■ The *Guide for Occupational Exploration:* Provides details on the 12 interest areas and the many jobs available within them.

2. Talk to people who already have jobs in your field of interest. Contact employers and make an appointment or ask questions over the telephone about what skills and training you would need in order for them to hire you. Talk to a guidance counselor at a high school, vocational or technical school, or college or university about the type of jobs you are interested in.

3. If you have access to the Internet, a lot of career information is available there. The *Occupational Outlook Handbook* lists some Internet sites, and you can also get career information and links to other sites by visiting JIST's site at http://www.jist.com.

If You Need More Training or Skills

What if you lack some of the skills or requirements for the job you want? Let's consider what your options are.

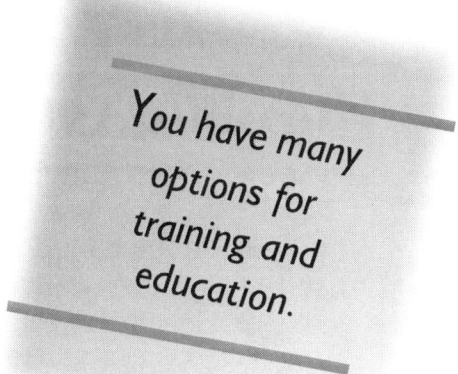

You have many options for training and education.

Formal Schooling

One option for gaining new skills or improving your skills is, of course, to go to school. There are many types of schools, such as colleges, universities, vocational, and technical schools. If you are thinking about entering a school program, here are some things to consider:

What Type of School Will Provide the Training You Need?

Some options are as follows:

- High school career training programs

- Community and junior colleges

- Four-year colleges and universities

- Vocational and technical schools

Identify Your Skills for School, Work, and Life

What Is the Reputation of the School?

Some things to check out:

- Does the school have good credentials?
- Do employers hire the school's graduates?

How Will You Pay for It?

Some options might be the following:

- Financial aid through the school or a government program
- Help from relatives or your employer
- Earning enough money by working while you go through the program
- Earn a scholarship

How Can You Arrange Your Schedule to Make Time for School?

You might have to do the following:

- Change jobs or change your work schedule
- Arrange for more child care if you have children
- Learn to manage your time better (get up earlier or go to bed later)

What Sacrifices Are You Willing to Make for School?

Be prepared to do the following:

- Give up some leisure time activities
- Give up things you might like to spend money on so that you can pay for school

- Set aside time for studying and homework
- Change your lifestyle

What Is the Location of the School That Best Suits Your Needs?

Can you do the following:

- Get to class meetings regularly?
- Move if necessary?

The Military

Another option for receiving training is the armed forces. You can enlist in the service and learn job skills that you can use for a civilian job when you have finished your tour of duty.

You can also qualify for scholarships and other forms of financial aid for career training programs and even university degrees.

Local recruitment offices can help you find information about career possibilities through the military. There are books such as *Military Careers* that are put out by the U.S. government.

These books contain information about available programs. Ask your librarian to help you locate this information.

On-the-Job Training

Some jobs do not require any formal training before you take the job. You learn by doing. This kind of job training can last from a few days to several years.

Your employer might place you under the supervision of another worker or send you to classes to train for the job.

You might also work toward a job you want in a business or organization by starting in an entry-level job. An entry-level job is often low skilled and low paying, but you can learn about the job you want to move up to. You can learn much about the organization and receive promotions if you do your work well.

Apprenticeships

An apprentice learns a trade by combining on-the-job training with classroom instruction. The program can last from one to six years.

Most programs are put on by employers, government programs, and labor unions. Bricklayers, auto mechanics, carpenters, and electricians are trade workers who learn their skills through an apprentice program.

Self-Directed Training

You can improve many skills by learning on your own. This is especially true of adaptive and transferable skills. Go back to Chapter Three and look over your checklists for these skills. On the lines that follow, write down again the skills that you want to improve.

_____

_____

_____

_____

_____

Choose the one that seems the most important right now. You should consider what will help you the most on the job you want when making your decision. Circle this skill or put a check mark next to it.

Use Your Outer Resources

There are many sources of help to improve the skill you have chosen. You could do the following things:

- Ask for help from a friend or relative who is good at that skill. ("Uncle Joe, you've always been so organized. How do you do it?")

- Find out about community programs in your area. High schools, hospitals, libraries, state universities, and many other organizations offer a wide range of adult programs on evenings and weekends. The cost is usually low.

    These programs cover both personal and practical skills. A few examples are as follows:

    - Learning math skills
    - Improving reading skills
    - Learning to use a computer
    - Learning how to be assertive

- Visit the library. A larger library will have many resources on education and training options and other career topics. Ask your librarian for help in finding what you need.

- Use the Internet. There are some great sites on the Internet to help young people plan their education, training, career, and life. You can find links to good sites via the major Internet service providers such as America Online. Or you can use a search engine like Yahoo.com to find other sites on topics that interest you.

Identify Your Skills for School, Work, and Life

Think About It

What are some other outer resources you might use?

_____

_____

_____

_____

Use Your Inner Resources

What inner resource is most important in developing your skills? Your attitude! If you believe you will succeed, your chances of doing so increase.

The opposite is also true. If you believe you won't succeed, you probably won't. Commit yourself to a positive attitude about your goals.

Stay Positive!
Put negative thoughts out of your mind every time they come in. This may take a lot of practice, but if you stick with it, it will become a habit. Commit yourself to a positive attitude about your goals.

76   © JIST Works, Inc., Indianapolis, IN

Chapter Five: Planning on How to Best Use Your Skills

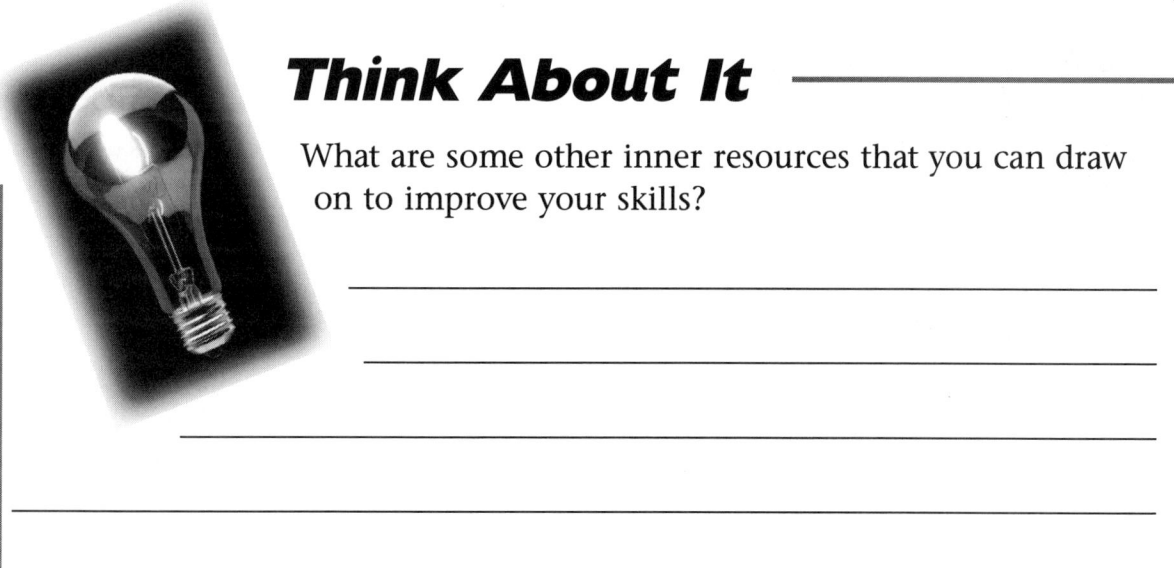

Think About It

What are some other inner resources that you can draw on to improve your skills?

_____

_____

_____

_____

Make a Plan

You have a better chance of reaching any goal you set if you do the following:

- Make the goal very specific.

- Decide on a plan to achieve the goal.

- Gather any information you need.

- Keep track of your progress.

- Find someone to be supportive and give you encouragement along the way.

- Stick with the plan and do it!

Did you know that Thomas Edison had to try hundreds of times before he designed a lightbulb that actually worked? That's a lot of "failures"! But his basic design made electricity popular and revolutionized our world. Success is often built on a series of failures.

In considering your education and career options, knowing what you *do not* want to do is just as important as what you *do* want to do. Planning isn't really about "failure" at all. It's about setting goals and finding ways to meet them. Edison did not fail hundreds of times, he continued to learn.

Goal Planning

This worksheet can help you make a plan to work on a skill you've decided to improve.

DIRECTIONS: Use this worksheet to set a goal and build a plan to make it happen.

Goal Planning Worksheet

Goal: _____

(Be specific. For example, "I will increase my word-processing speed to 60 words per minute by June of this year.")

Information I Will Gather	Do It By

People I Need to Talk To	Do It By

Chapter Five: Planning on How to Best Use Your Skills

What I Need to Do/How I Will Do It	Do It By

Days and times I will study or practice this skill or parts of this skill:

Day	Skill	Time
Monday		
Tuesday		

(continued)

Identify Your Skills for School, Work, and Life

Goal Planning Worksheet (continued)

Day	Skill	Time
Wednesday		
Thursday		
Friday		
Saturday		

Day	Skill	Time
Sunday		

Measure Your Progress

When you were a child, how did you know you were growing? Maybe someone marked your height on the wall, and each time the mark was higher than the last time. Or maybe you noticed that you could reach the faucet in the sink without using a stool.

It helps to see real results. Keeping track of your progress keeps you motivated.

Some ways to keep track of your progress are as follows:

- Buy a calendar to use only for your progress record keeping.
- Keep a journal.
- Use index cards and keep them organized.
- Use a computer program designed for tracking and record keeping. You'll be practicing a valuable skill while you're logging your own progress.
- Use a tape recorder as a spoken journal. Start each new entry with the date, and tell what you accomplished, how you did it, and how you feel about it. Talk about obstacles and how you will or how you did handle them.

Checkpoint

After completing this chapter, answer these questions. They will help you review what you just learned.

1. What are some ways to get information about jobs?

_____
_____
_____
_____
_____

2. Are failures good or bad? Why?

_____
_____
_____
_____
_____

3. What can you learn from risking failure?

_____
_____
_____
_____
_____

Chapter Five: Planning on How to Best Use Your Skills

4. How does tracking your progress help you improve your skills?

_____

_____

_____

_____

_____

Notes

Write down any questions you have about what you read. Or make notes about points you want to remember.

Identify Your Skills for School, Work, and Life

CHALLENGE:
Focus on Goals and Strategies

Try to imagine your life ten years from now. What kind of person do you want to be? Where do you want to be living? How would you like friends, family, and coworkers to describe you? Write your answers in the spaces here.

_____

_____

_____

_____

_____

_____

_____

_____

_____

_____

_____

Chapter Five: Planning on How to Best Use Your Skills

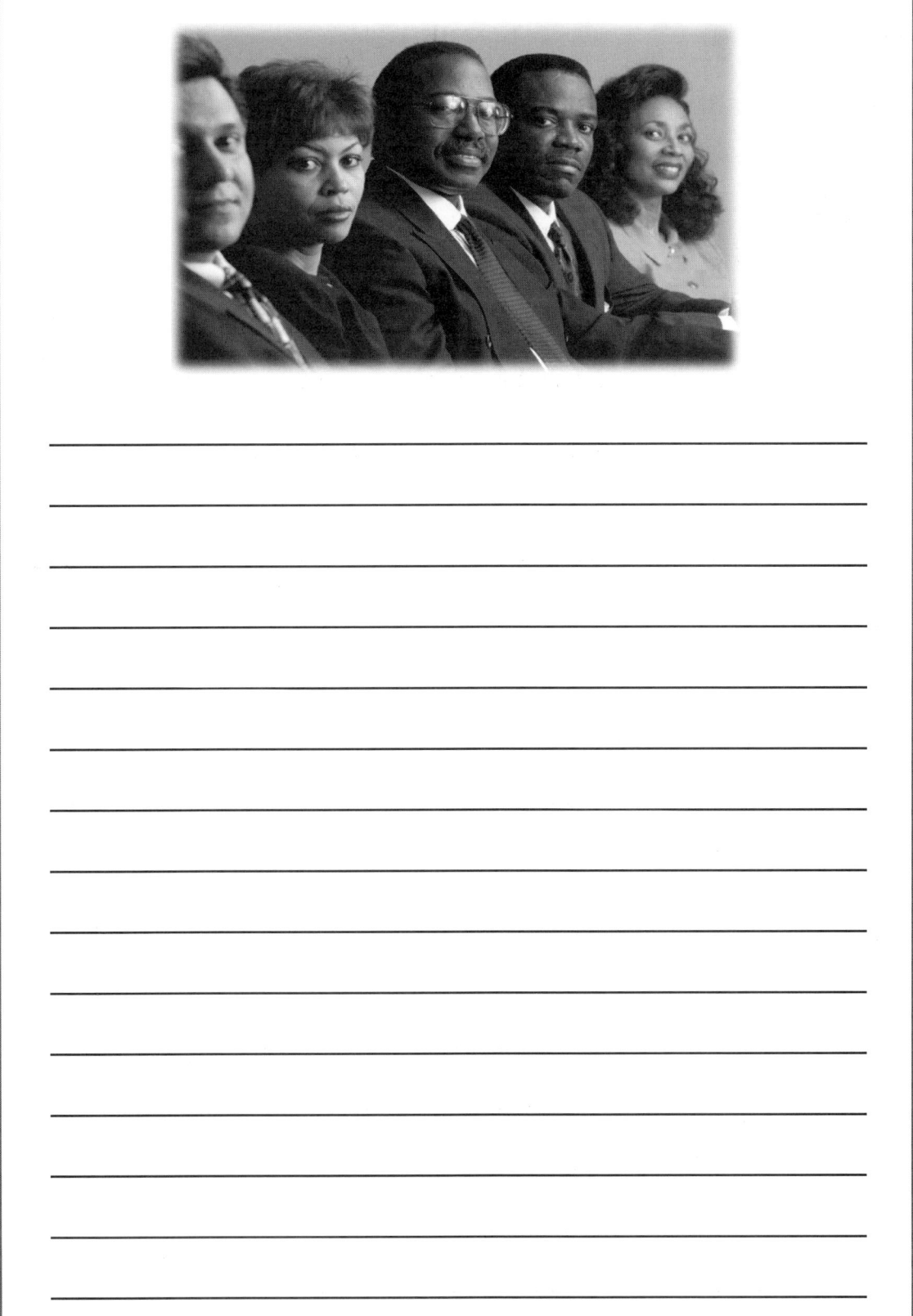

Conclusion
Skills for Life

Congratulations!

By completing this book, you have taken the first step in taking control of your life. You will also be taking responsibility for everything that happens—and doesn't happen—to you.

Knowing what you can do, what you want to do, and how to do it is a big part of being successful in whatever you do.

This book about identifying your skills can help with the first step—the rest is up to you. Make the most of your skills, and your dreams can come true.

Good luck!

Call 1-800-648-JIST today!

JIST's Job Search Basics Series

by J. Michael Farr & Susan Christophersen

Four Key Job Search Topics—Each in Its Own Workbook

Looking for a job is a challenge. JIST's Job Search Basics series makes it easier. Each workbook covers just one essential topic, so you get clear, complete advice that will help you find a good job in less time.

After introducing the topic, the workbooks help you practice what you've learned through worksheets and special features called Think About It, Checkpoint, and Challenge. Examples often feature a talk between two people about someone's job search. You learn what works—and what doesn't—with these real-world discussions.

Used together, these workbooks give you the big picture on starting and succeeding in your job search.

Each workbook just $7.95

Identify Your Skills for School, Work, and Life
Second Edition

Helps you identify your skills. Guides you in creating a skills inventory from all your experiences.

ISBN 1-56370-583-4
Order Code J583-4

Introduction to Job Applications
Second Edition

Explains how to fill in application forms. Helps you develop the information you will need to complete applications.

ISBN 1-56370-581-8
Order Code J581-8

Two Best Ways to Find a Job
Second Edition

Shows how to use "warm" and "cold" contacts to find a job. Helps you find the unadvertised "hidden" job market.

ISBN 1-56370-580-X
Order Code J580-X

Why Should I Hire You?: Turn Interview Questions into Job Offers
Second Edition

Explains how to sell yourself to employers. Lets you practice the three-step process for answering interview questions.

ISBN 1-56370-582-6
Order Code J582-6